LES REFLETS DE L'OBSCURITÉ

for Classical Guitar

I0795258

Josquin Schwizgebel

for Johan Smith

Winner-Guitar Foundation of America
International Competition 2019

Cover Photograph courtesy of ESA / Hubble. Used by Permission.

WWW.MELBAY.COM

TABLES DES MATIÈRES

NOTES TECHNIQUES

Dans ce recueil, les altérations (♯♮♭) tiennent durant toute la durée de l'encadré ou d'un groupe de notes reliées entre elles.

La plupart du temps, la notation rythmique est indicative. L'interprète veillera à relier les éléments dans des courbes dynamiques, souples et harmonieuses.

Chaque encadré représente une trajectoire musicale directionnelle ou cyclique à relier avec l'évènement suivant.

Afin de simplifier l'écriture, l'expansion du son n'a pas été écrite. Cependant, il est souhaitable de laisser, dans la mesure du possible, les notes s'éteindre naturellement.

Enfin, le minutage est relatif et tolère une certaine flexibilité si cela sert l'expression musicale.

TECHNICAL NOTES

In this collection, the alterations (♯♮♭) hold for the entire duration of the boxset or a group of related notes.

Most of the time, the rhythmic notation is indicative. The performer should take care to connect the elements in dynamic, flexible and harmonious curves.

Each boxset represents a directional or cyclical musical trajectory which should be linked to the next section.

In order to simplify the writing, the sound expansion has not been written. However, it is desirable to let the notes fade naturally as far as possible.

Finally, timing is relative and allows for flexibility should it serve musical expression.

Avec l'aimable soutien des Fondations

NICATI - DE LUZE

Fondation ABπ

Crédits Photo : "*Star Cluster R136*" - NASA, ESA and P.Crowther (University of Sheffield)

TEXTES D'ACCOMPAGNEMENT

Secrets d'une ombre

Dans l'obscurité ou la lumière, la chaleur ou le froid, chaque histoire a son aurore… et son crépuscule. Avant le tout est le rien. Puis soudain, une étincelle et l'existence commence. Aux confins de l'Univers, dans l'ombre d'un corps matériel, naît la vie.

In darkness or light, heat or cold, each story has its dawn... and its dusk. Before Everything there is Nothing. Then, suddenly, a spark flies and existence begins. At the ends of the universe, in the shadows of a material body, life springs.

I - Ecume orange

Je suis là… ici… Mais personne ne me répond. Seule, sans vie, je me perds. Mon corps, dénué de substance, dérive au son des vagues de l'amertume. Quel est cet endroit ?

Parfois, au gré des ondoiements de la matière, je vois un reflet s'esquisser, un souvenir affleurer. Sans pouvoir m'en saisir. Depuis combien de temps suis-je ici, suspendue entre les strates de l'horizon ? L'obscurité me berce, me serre, m'étouffe.

Au loin, un éclat. L'océan de néant devient un océan de possibles. Je me rapproche de la lueur nimbant les vagues. Je glisse, je m'étends, je fusionne. Mon essence se teinte d'une douce nuance et se réchauffe. Mes longs bras s'étirent autour de moi. Le vent furieux vient à ma rencontre et me donne l'impulsion pour me détacher de cet enfer liquide qui pourtant me compose.

Et je m'élance…

I am here... right here... But no one answers me. Alone, bereft of life, I lose myself. My body, stripped of its substance, drifts to the sound of waves of bitterness. What is this place ?

Sometimes, in time with the undulations of matter, I see a reflection begin to appear and a memory surfaces without me being able to take hold. How long have I been here, suspended within the long rays of the horizon? Darkness rocks me, holds me fast, chokes me.

In the distance, a spark springs to life. This ocean of nothingness becomes an ocean of possiblity. I move closer to the shimmering light on the waves. I slide, I stretch out, I melt. The essence of my being softens and warms. My long arms lengthen around me. Furious winds blow towards me and shakes me loose from this liquid hell, though it is a part of me.

And I take flight...

II - Parfums d'éclipse

Je ne suis plus que sensations. Dispersée dans les airs, embrassée par le souffle du vent. Mes perles de lumière s'égayent et dansent à l'infini, toujours plus haut dans la tempête, vers cet horizon qui m'appelle et me transforme. Puis, cette chaleur me quitte alors qu'une sphère pâle s'interpose et m'arrache aux rayons astraux. Je me sens déchirée, privée d'un nouveau type d'oxygène. Je crie, hurle et me débats à l'intérieur. Mais personne ne m'entend.

À l'ombre du monde, alors que le goût de la perte submerge tout mon être, l'odeur de l'inconnu m'enivre.

Je décroche.

All that is left of me is sensation, feeling. I am scattered in the air and borne up by a breath of wind. The beads of light that I am become enlivened with joy and dance into infinity, ever higher in the storm, towards the horizon that beckons and transforms me. Then, my warmth leaves me, as a pale sphere appears and tears me away from the astral beams. I feel as though I have been ripped apart and deprived of a new kind of oxygen. I cry out, I scream and struggle to break loose on the inside. But no one hears me.

In the shadow of the world, with the taste of loss overwhelming my entire being, the smell of the unknown intoxicates me.

I let go.

III - Sables stellaires

Emportée par mon élan, je continue à m'élever.

Un écho me parvient. Une douce mélopée égrenée par un corps froid jadis nommé *Voyager* trace un sillon de quiétude au loin. Ses accents mélodieux et calmes me renvoient à un lointain passé, à une existence différente. Mon regard s'abîme dans une éternité dont les millions d'étoiles scintillent seules dans un vaste océan d'ébène qui s'effondre.

Un vertige et soudain, je m'emballe. Je tournoie et je chavire dans ce gouffre sans fin qu'est l'espace céleste. Une multitude de sphères de lumière se déforment sur mon passage, des murmures envahissent mes pensées. Puis plus rien. Je flotte. Je dérive au milieu d'une pouponnière d'étoiles. Je suis l'une d'elles. Un point parmi tant d'autres, une petite constellation improbable et sans nom, qui contemple un monde en fusion évoluer autour d'elle, à l'infini.

Maintenant, je sais.

Borne away by my momentum, I rise higher and higher.

An echo reaches me. A gentle strain hummed by a cold body which was once named *Voyager* traces a channel of tranquility in the distance. Its melodious and calm tones remind me of a far-away past, a different existence. My gaze dives into an eternity whose millions of stars that shine alone and make up a vast and collapsing ocean of jet black.

A feeling of dizziness and suddenly, I take off. I spin around in this endless abyss of celestial space. Countless spheres of light change shape as I move past them and murmurs invade my thoughts. And then, nothing. I float. I drift through a nursery of stars. I am one of them. One dot among so many others, a small unlikely and unnamed constellation contemplating a molten world that is infinitely evolving around it.

Now, I know.

Textes d'accompagnement écrits par Anne Gauthier
Traduction anglaise par Alisa Steinhauser

Secrets d'une ombre

Josquin Schwizgebel
Octobre 2019

A **Léger & Enigmatique**

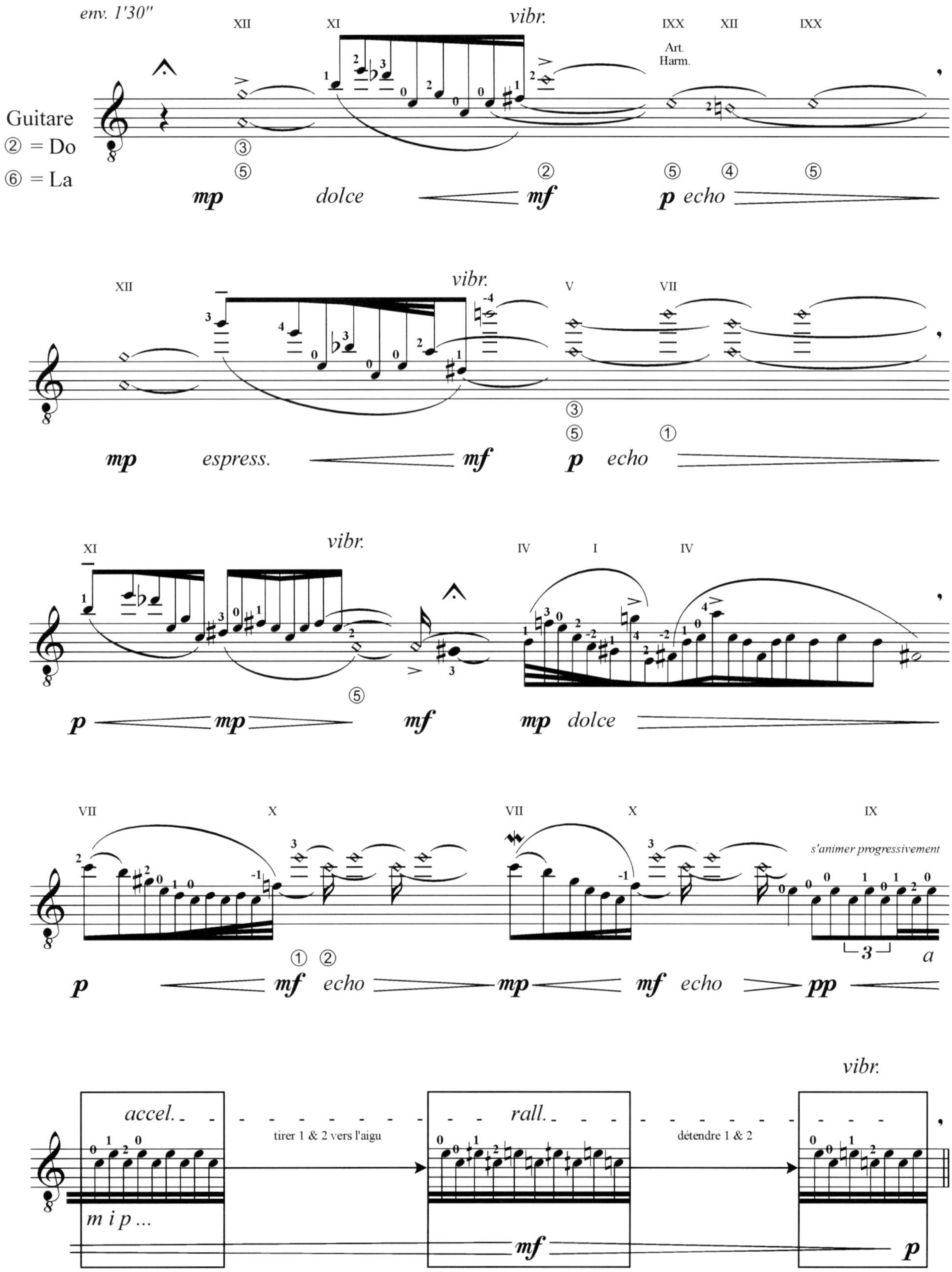

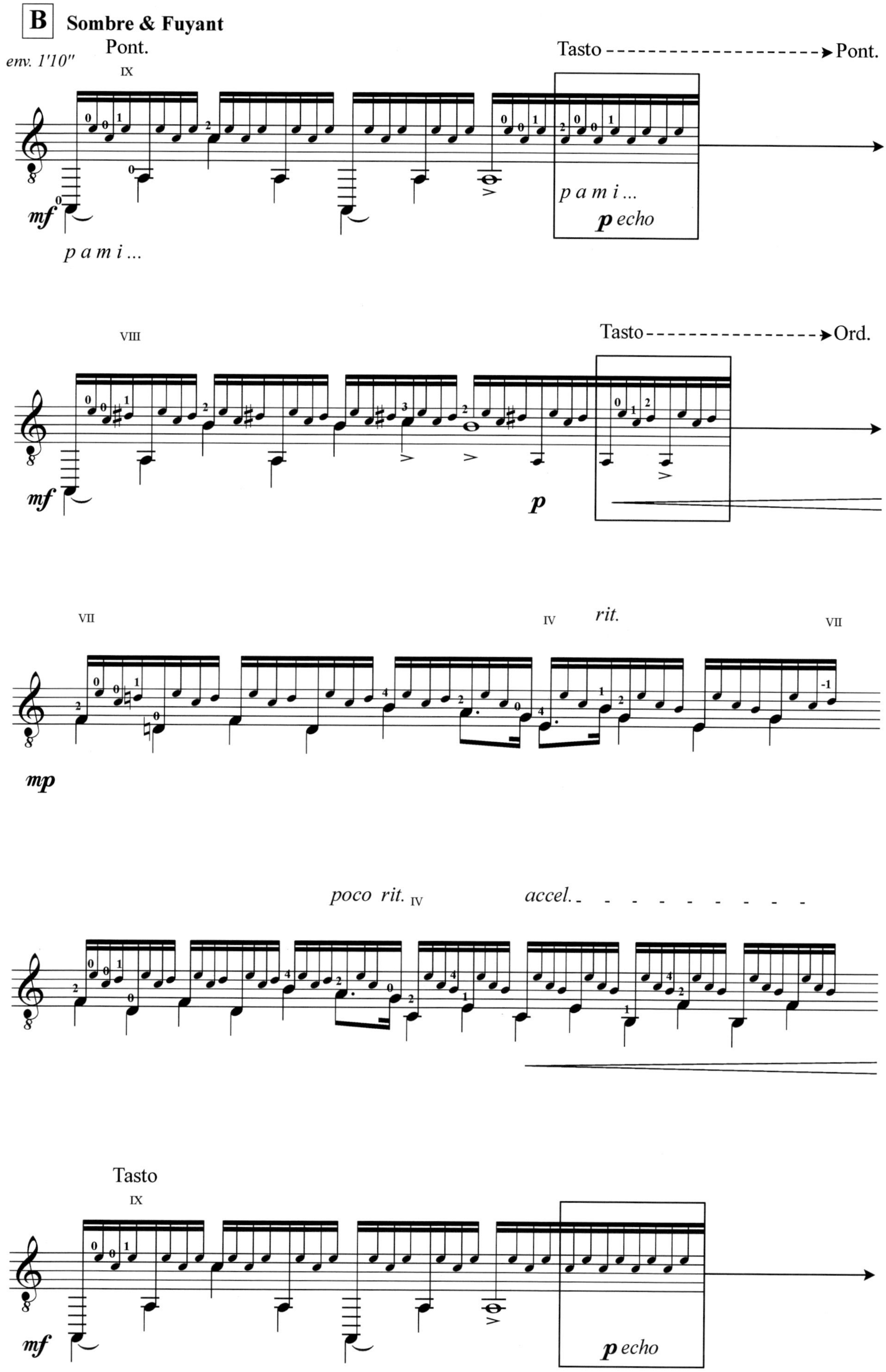
B
Sombre & Fuyant
env. 1'10"
Pont.
IX
Tasto
Pont.
mf
p a m i ...
p echo
VIII
Tasto
Ord.
p
VII
IV
rit.
VII
mp
poco rit.
IV
accel.
Tasto
IX
mf
p echo

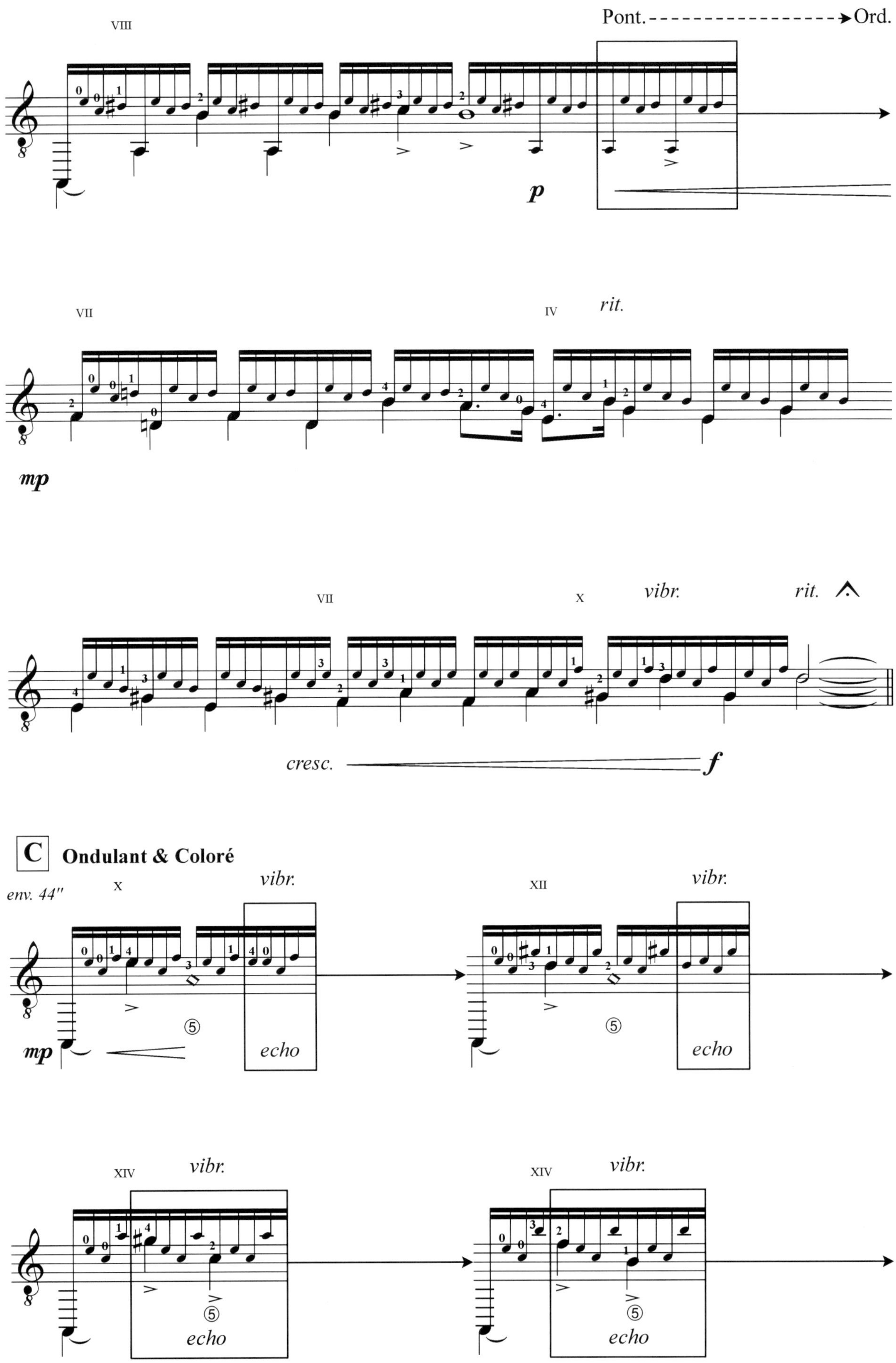
VIII
Pont. ------------------> Ord.
p
VII
IV
rit.
mp
VII
X
vibr.
rit.
cresc.
f
C
Ondulant & Coloré
env. 44"
X
vibr.
mp
echo
XII
vibr.
echo
XIV
vibr.
echo
XIV
vibr.
echo

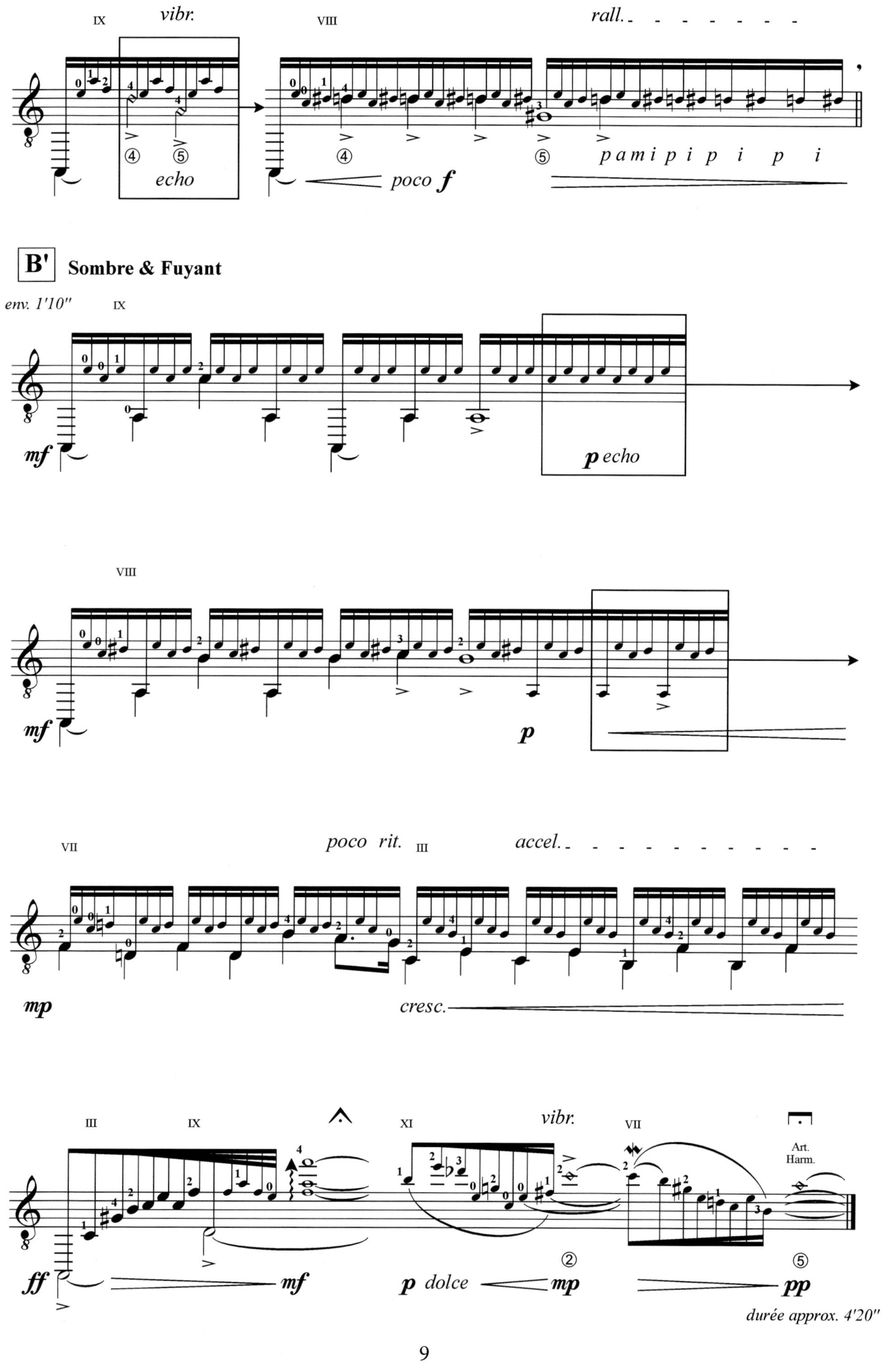
IX
vibr.
VIII
rall.
echo
poco f
p a m i p i p i p i
B'
Sombre & Fuyant
env. 1'10"
mf
p echo
VIII
mf
p
VII
poco rit.
III
accel.
mp
cresc.
III
IX
XI
vibr.
VII
Art.
Harm.
ff
mf
p dolce
mp
pp
durée approx. 4'20"

I - Ecume orange

Josquin Schwizgebel
Octobre 2019

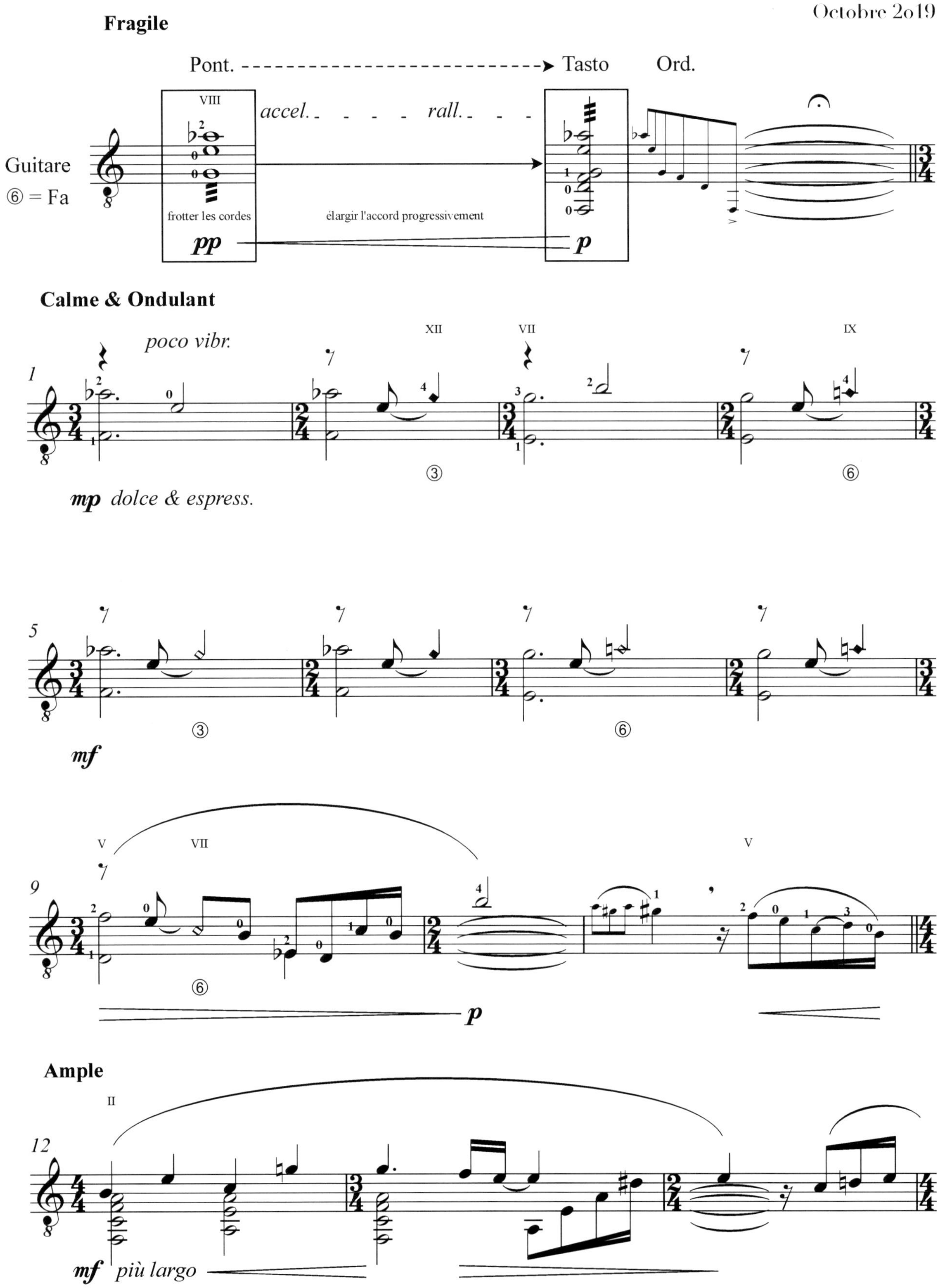

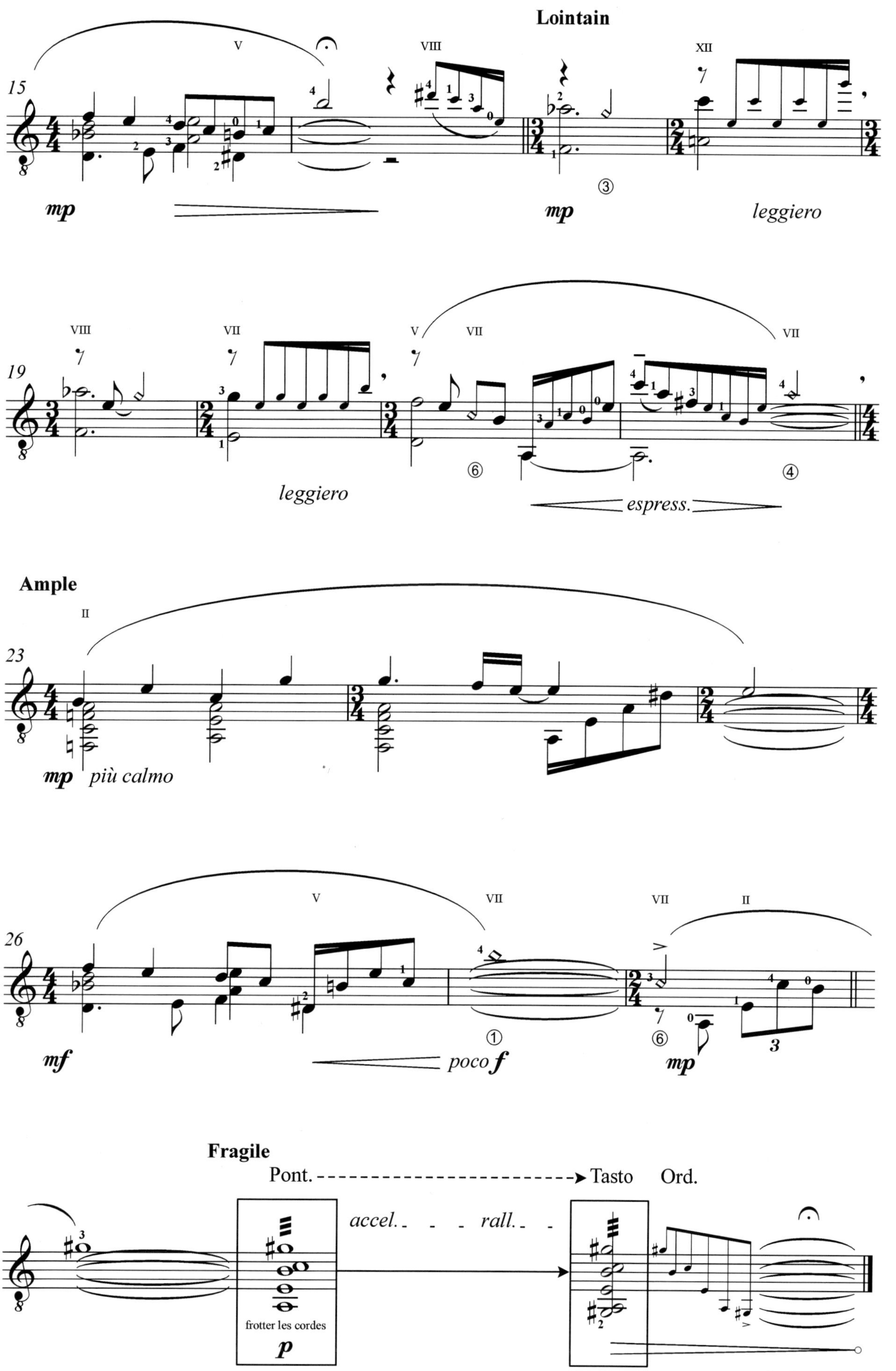

durée approx. 2'30"

II - Parfums d'éclipse

Josquin Schwizgebel
Octobre 2019

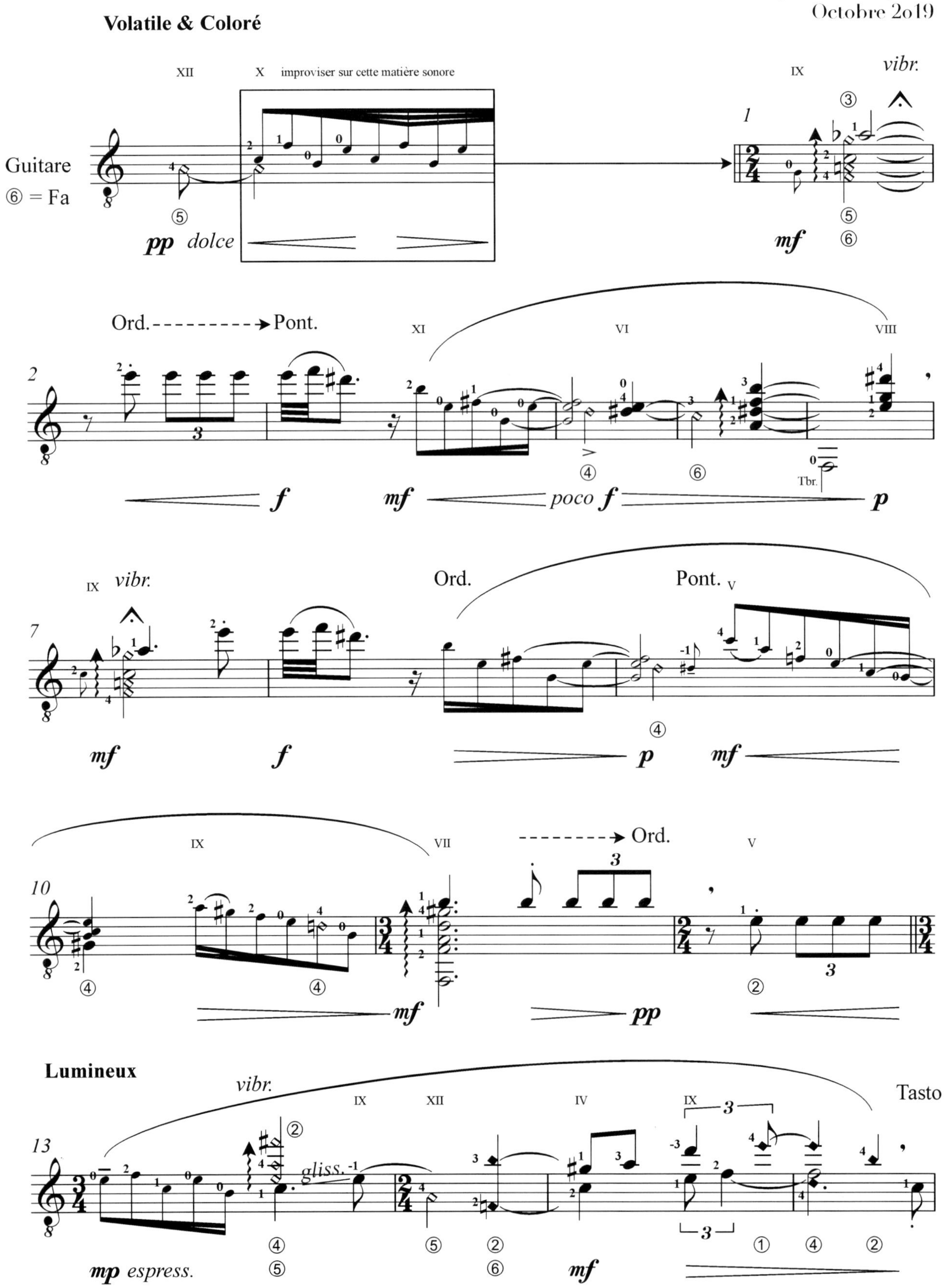

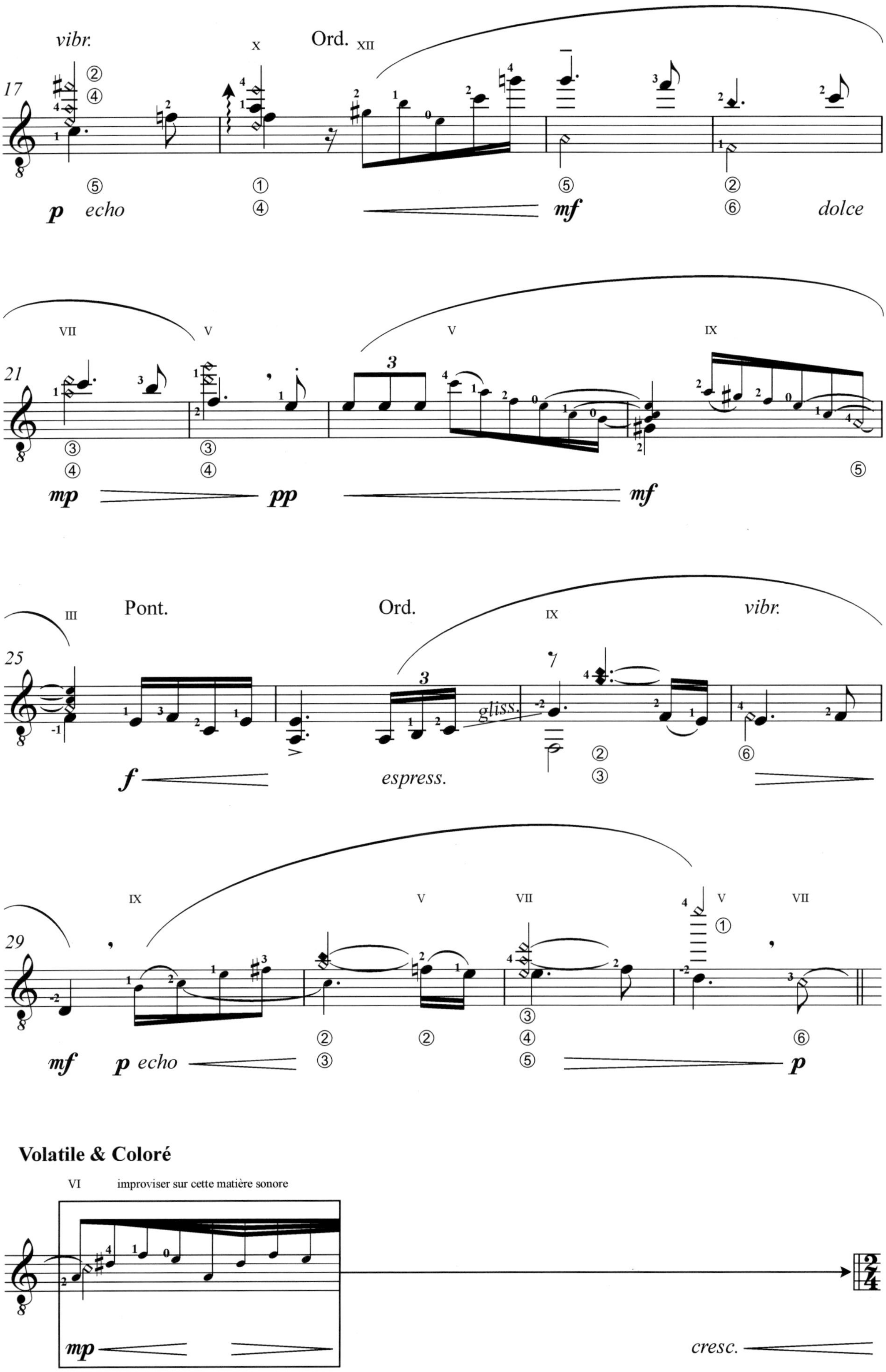
vibr.
Ord.
p echo
mf
dolce
mp
pp
mf
Pont.
Ord.
vibr.
gliss.
f
espress.
mf
p echo
p
Volatile & Coloré
improviser sur cette matière sonore
mp
cresc.

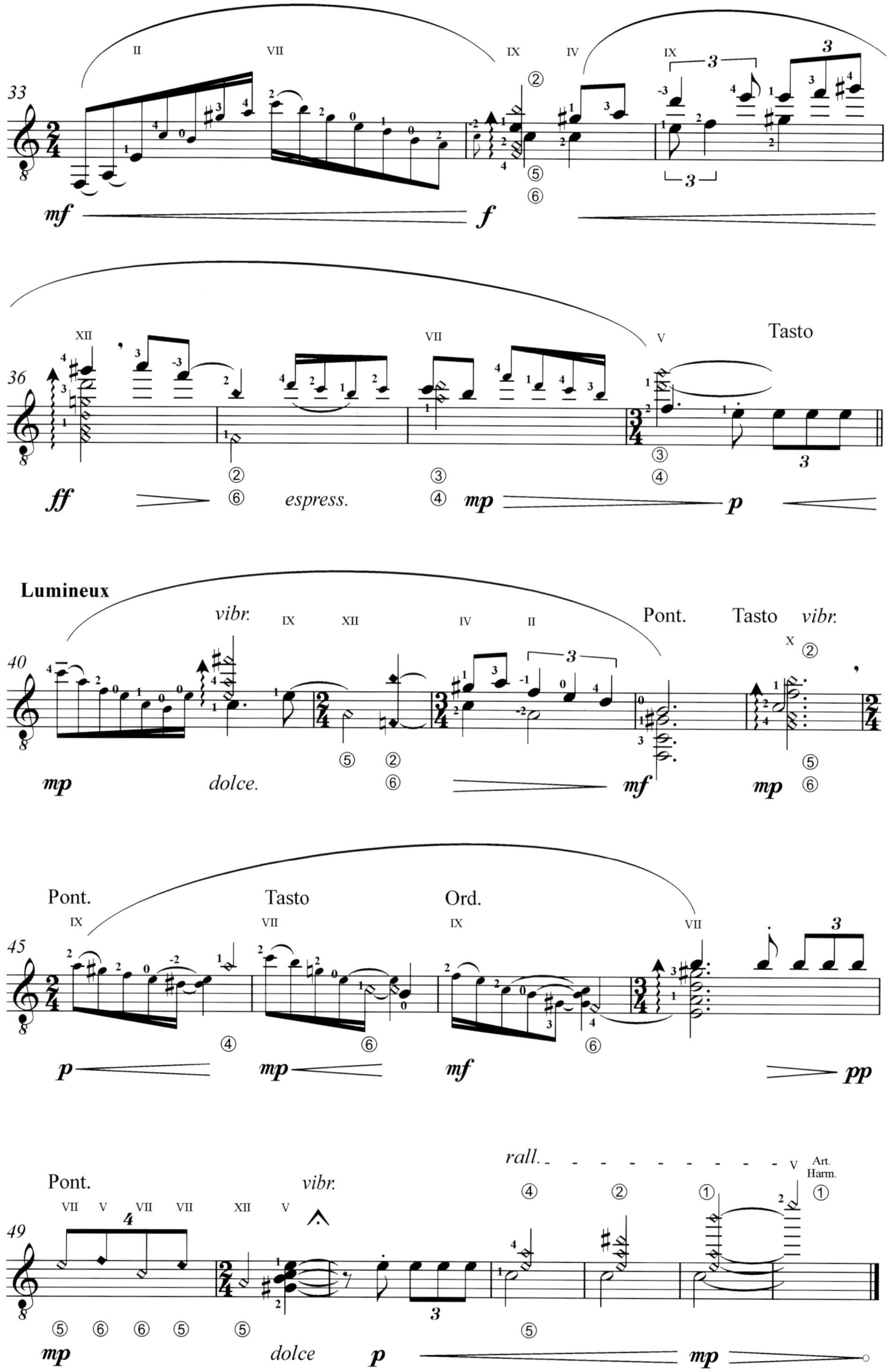

durée approx. 3'20''

III - Sables stellaires

Josquin Schwizgebel
Octobre 2019

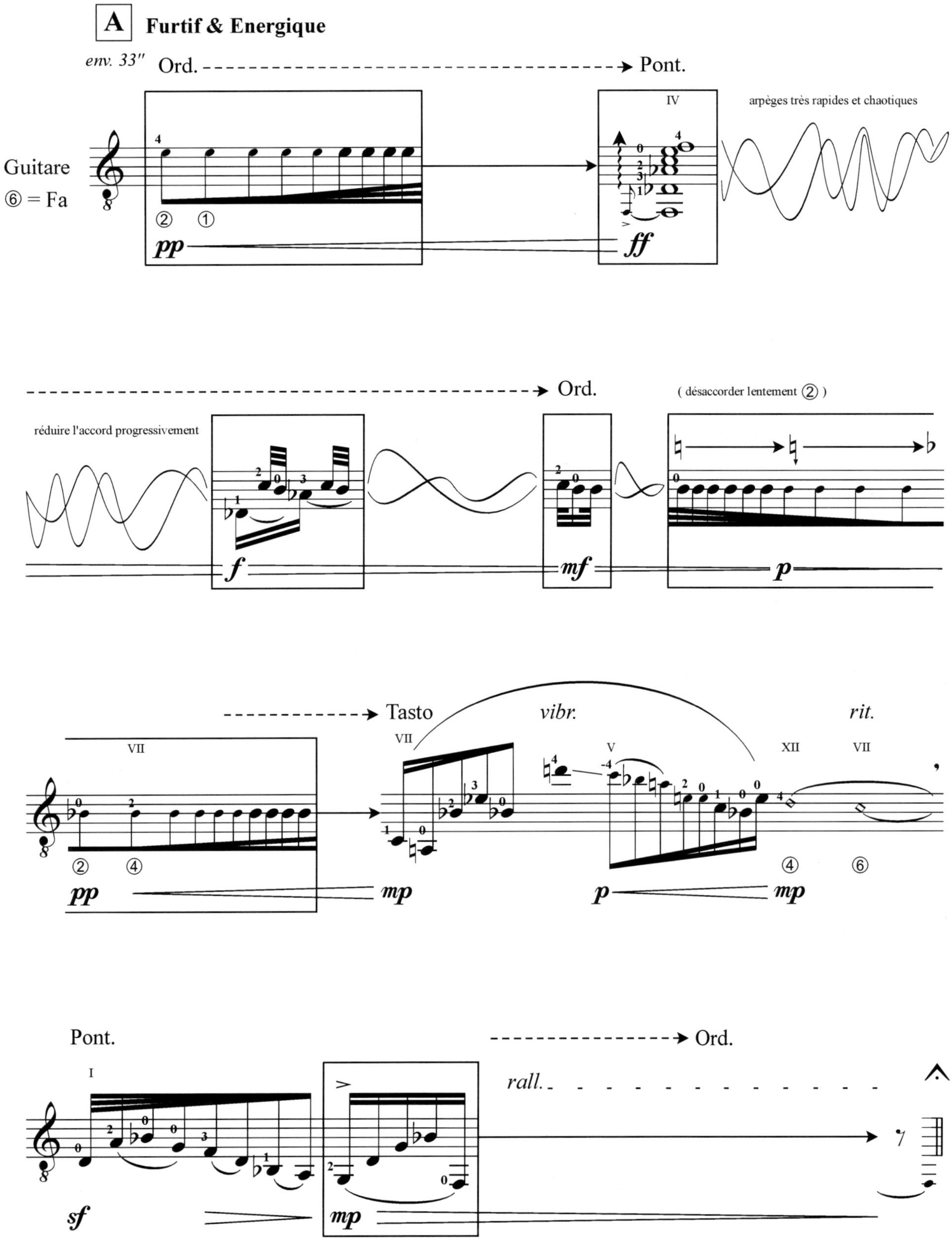

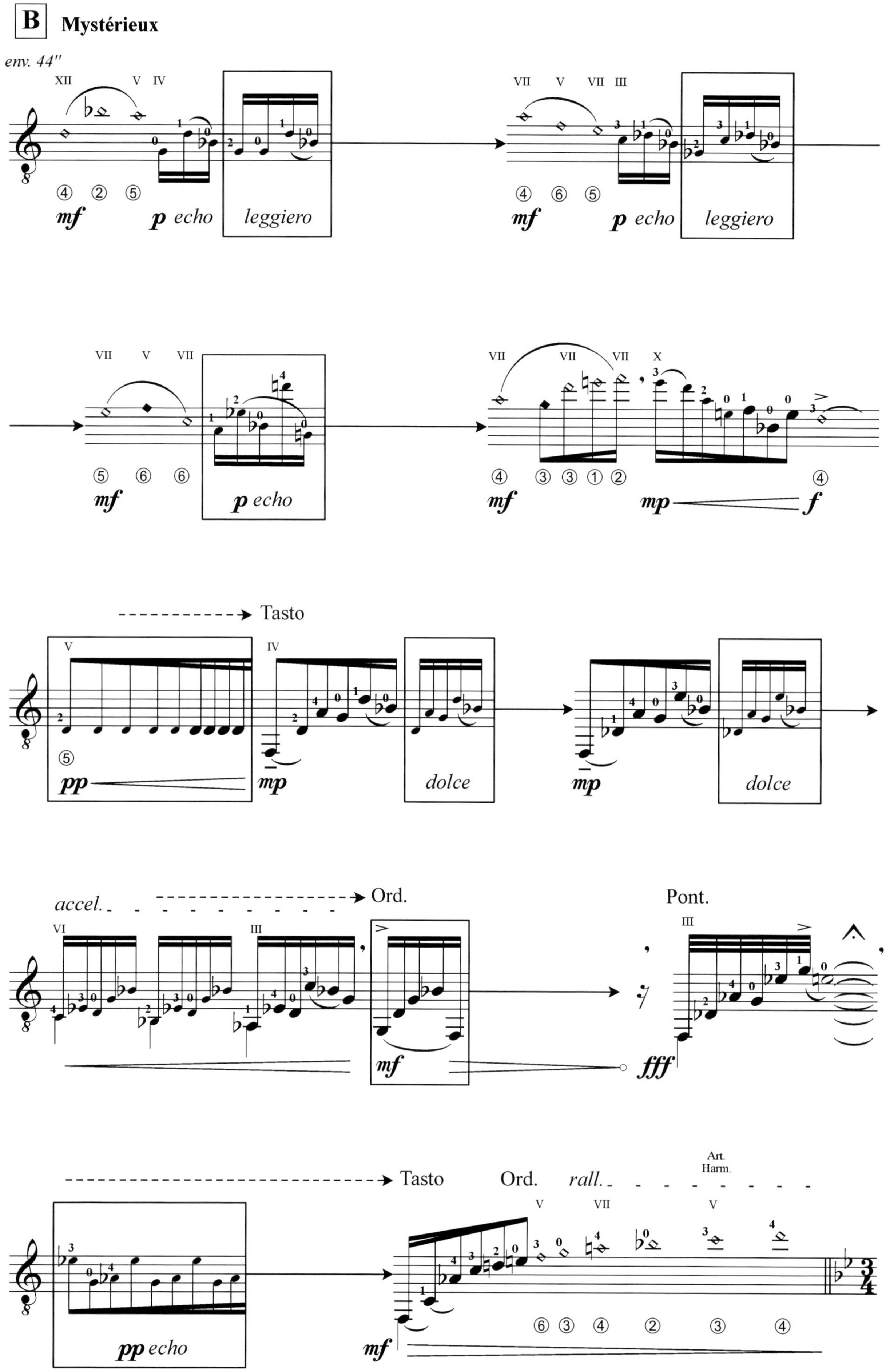
B
Mystérieux
env. 44''
mf
p echo
leggiero
mf
p echo
leggiero
mf
p echo
mf
mp
f
Tasto
pp
mp
dolce
mp
dolce
accel.
Ord.
mf
Pont.
fff
Tasto
Ord.
rall.
Art. Harm.
pp echo
mf

C Nostalgique

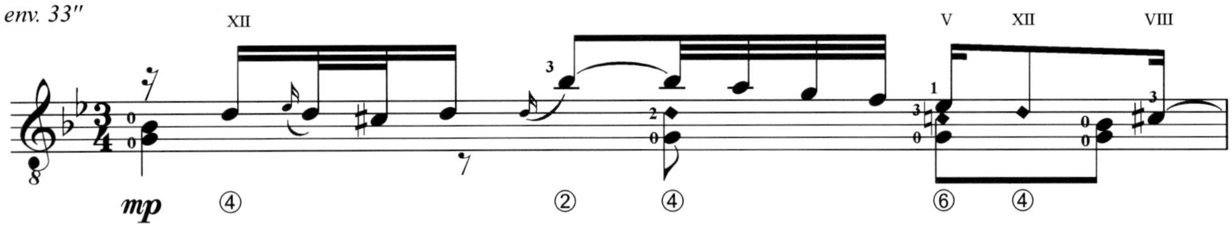

J.S. Bach - BWV 988 Variation No.25

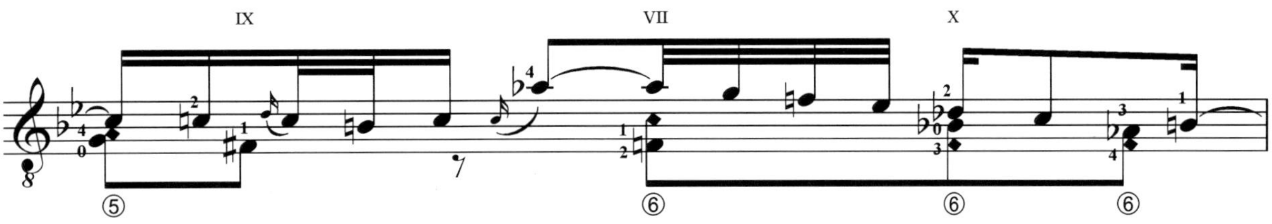

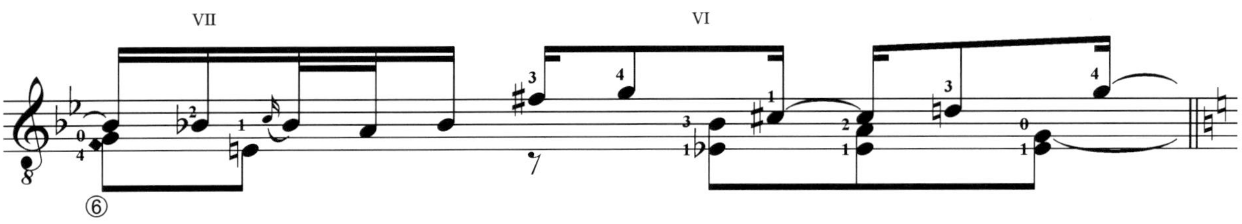

B Lointain

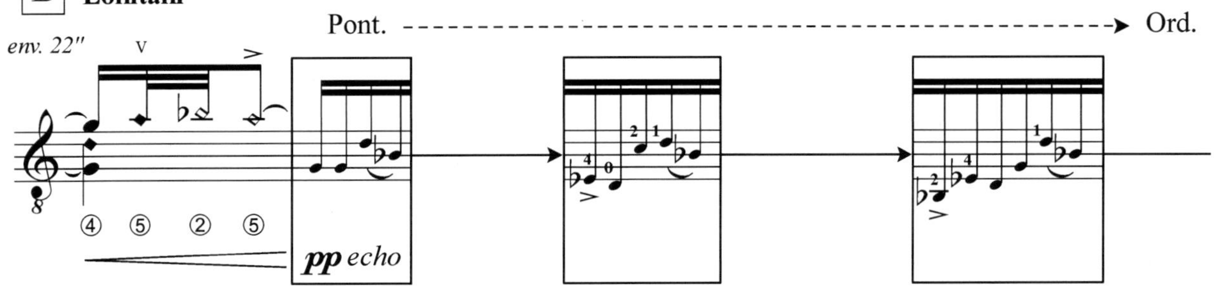

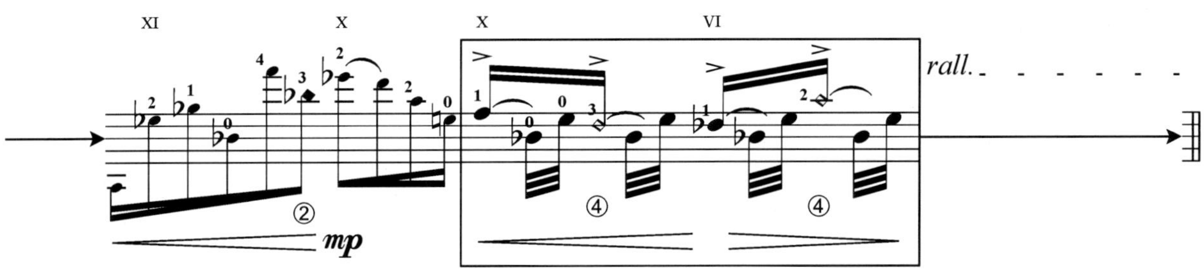

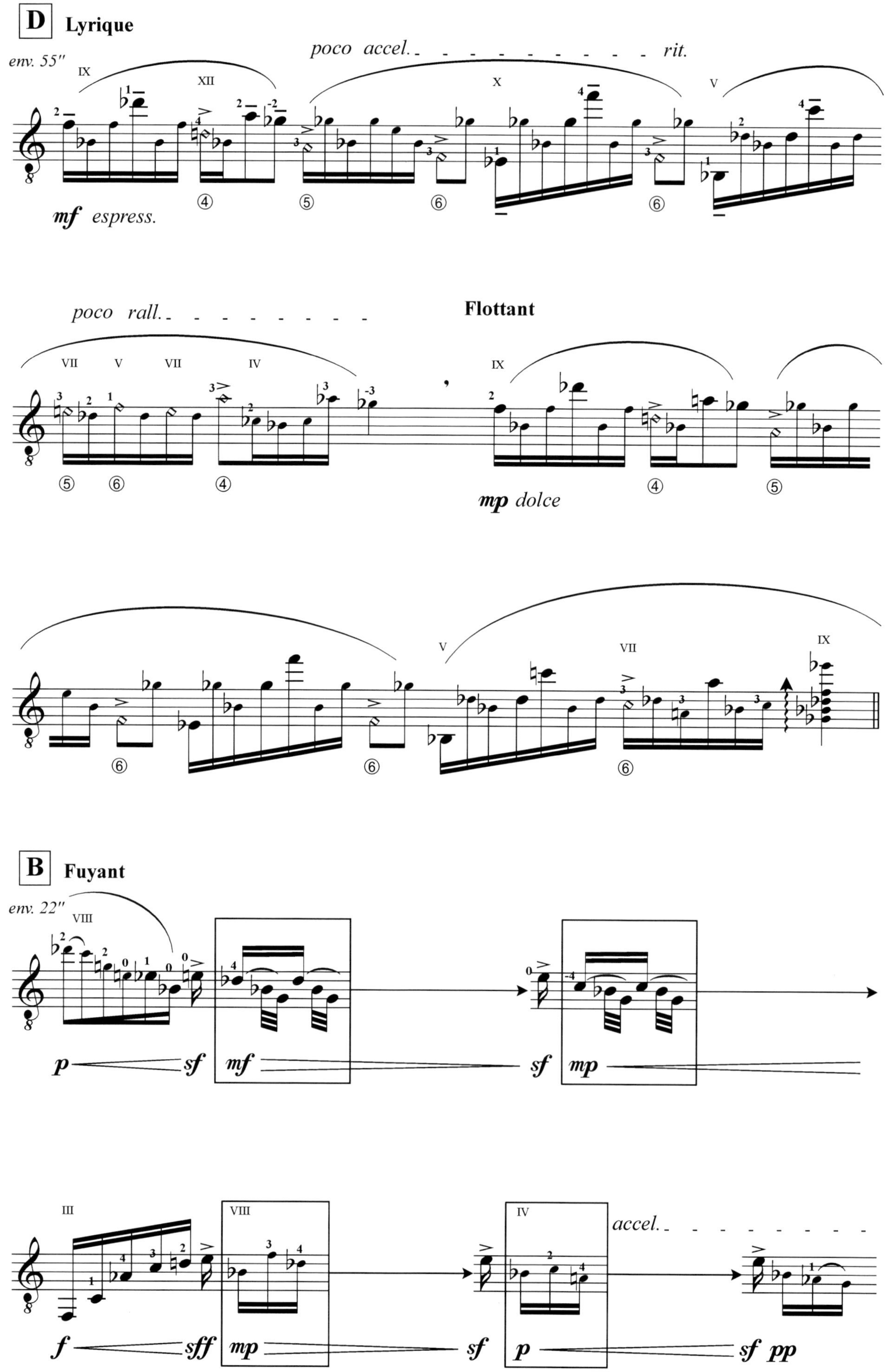
D Lyrique
env. 55″
poco accel.
rit.
mf espress.
poco rall.
Flottant
mp dolce
B Fuyant
env. 22″
p
sf
mf
sf
mp
f
sff
mp
sf
p
accel.
sf pp

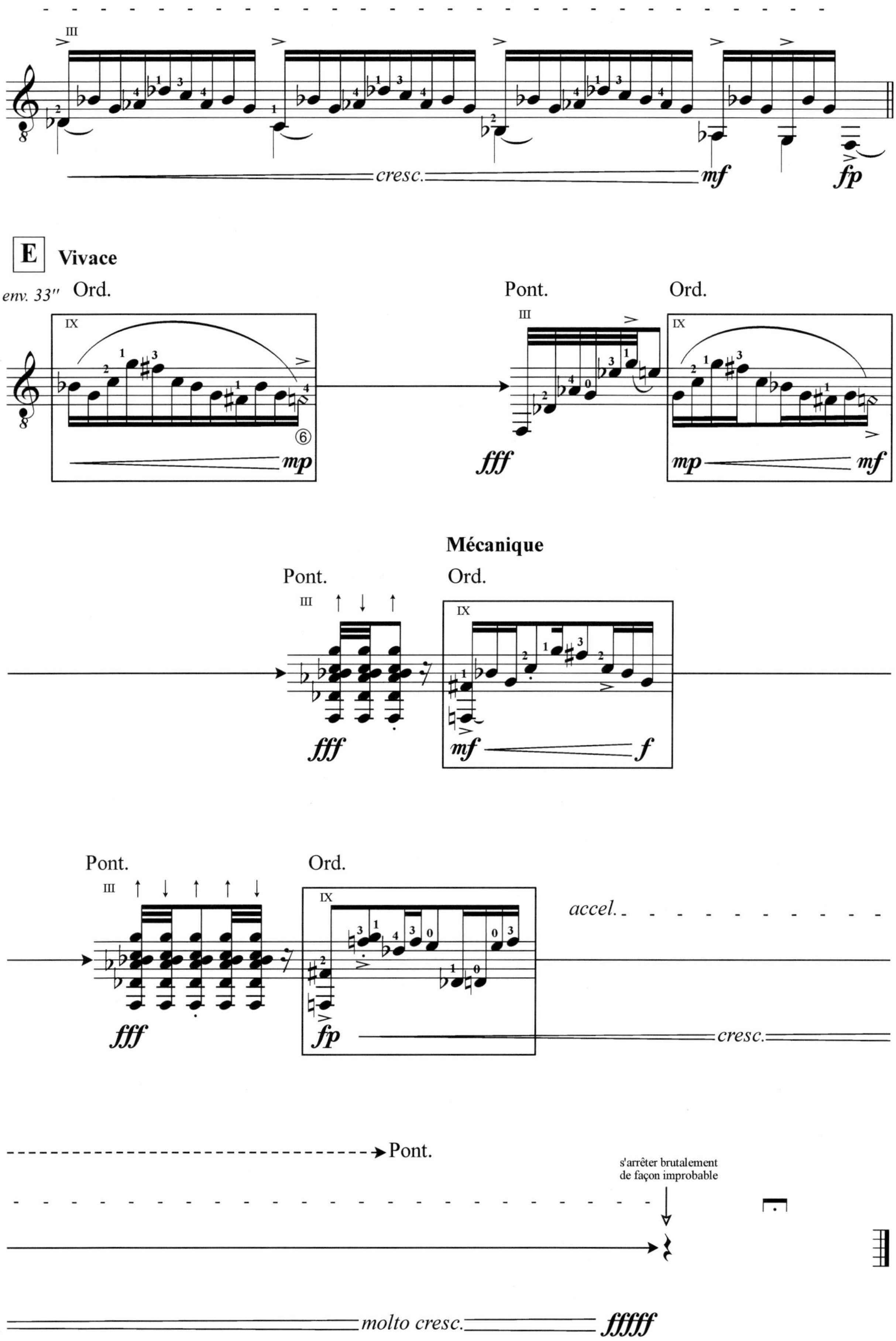

durée approx. 4'20"

Josquin Schwizgebel - *Photo by Marie-France Millasson*

JOSQUIN SCHWIZGEBEL

Composition

After having successfully trained as a plasterer and painter, Josquin signed up to study as a professional electric guitar player at EJMA (Ecole de Jazz et de Musique Actuelle in Lausanne). However, after a series of events, he decided to change to classical music studies a year later as a student of Dagoberto Linhares at Lausanne's HEMU (Haute Ecole de Musique). This contrasting turn in music allowed him to diversify and enrich his musical sound palette. To further widen the scope of musical discovery, Josquin decided to spend a year studying at Berlin's Hochschule für Musik Hanns Eisler. Having returned to Switzerland, he obtained his BA and MA in musical education in the class of George Vassilev, while also taking courses in composition with William Blank.

Strongly encouraged by his professors, Josquin went on the study for his MA in composition in 2015 under Xavier Dayer at Bern University of the Arts (HKB), obtaining his degree in September 2018. Josquin continues to cultivate and develop his musical creativity by composing and collaborating on a regular basis with various musicians and groups, whose styles range from jazz to baroque music.

Josquin plays the guitar as part of Mérion (a two guitar and violin trio), whose musical repertoire consists entirely of pieces composed by him. His musical sensitivity combines darkness and depth with a luminous touch to produce a musical immersion in an original and poetic universe.

As a parallel to his creative work, Josquin teaches classical guitar at musical academies in Vevey (CMVR) and Yverdon (CMNV).

To this day, Josquin's projects have taken a combination of diverse paths such as : *Les reflets de l'obscurité* (2019) - pieces for solo guitar performed by Johan Smith on tour in North America, China and Switzerland ; *Les dentelles du cygne* (2019) and *Les vestiges d'une galaxie* (2018) - pieces performed in Europe by George Vassilev and Irina-Kalina Goudeva ; *Ballade dans un néant controversé* (2018) - performed by the ensemble Polytheistic Tema from Karlsruhe ; *L'araignée ivre* (2017) - piece for 100 musicians ; *Construire sur un nuage* (2017) - performed by the ensemble Proton ; a dozen pieces for a string ensemble commissioned as part of Julien Vergère's performance « Avec Elle » and recorder at L'Heure bleue in La Chaux-de-Fonds (2017) ; several acousmatic pieces created using sound samples from around the world, among which *Ping-Pong sur Amukta* (2017), *Départ en ozone, Vide raisonnant, Derniers instants* (2016) *Une façon de mourir* (2015) and *L'atelier en bois* (2014).

In 2020 Josquin is working on a collaboration with Parisian writer Julie Ménard for the Dutch ensemble Asko Schönberg, to be performed at the Festival d'Avignon.

www.josquinschwizgebel.com

Johan Smith - *Photo by Luca Vimercati*

JOHAN SMITH

Guitar

Winner of the prestigious *Guitar Foundation of America (GFA)* competition in 2019 and defined as the *"Classical Guitar Revelation 2017"* by the french magazine *"Guitar Classical Magazine"*, Johan Smith has been invited to perform in renowned festivals, as concert and soloist, with orchestras such as the *Budapest Symphony Orchestra,* the *Lausanne Chamber Orchestra* and the *Verbier Festival Orchestra*. He is currently preparing the recording of his second album (*Naxos,* 2020), as well as a tour that will bring him to perform in China, the United States, Canada, Mexico, and at the Carnegie Hall in New York.

His particular interest in contemporary music has led him to collaborate with several composers, including Josquin Schwizgebel and Arnaud Fillion who dedicated him his *"Concerto for Guitar and Orchestra"*, created in Budapest in 2019.

In addition to the *Guitar Foundation of America,* Johan Smith won prizes in the following competitions: 1st prize at the 8th *Changsha International Guitar Competition* (China), Special Prize from the *Victoria & Joaquin Rodrigo Foundation,* 1st prize at the 6th *International Guitar Competion of Thessaloniki,* 1st prize at the *International Competition of Fontenay-Sous-Bois,* 1st prize at the 5th *International Festival Guitare au Beffroi,* 1st prize at the 89th *Leopold Bellan International Competition,* 1st prize at the 13th *National Competition of Ceyzeriat* (also winning the public prize), 3rd prize at the 3rd *Pleven International Guitar Competition,* 3rd prize at the 1st *Aalborg International Guitar Competition*.

Born in 1990 in Geneva, Johan obtained a Bachelor in 2015 and a *"Master of Arts in Instrumental Pedagogy"* in 2017 at the University of Music of Lausanne, in the class of Dagoberto Linhares. In addition to this activity as a guitar teacher at the Conservatory of Morges, he also obtained in 2019 the most important academic title in the field of musical performance in Switzerland: the *"Master of Arts specializing in Music Performance Soloist"*, awarded by the highest grade.

In a completely different approach, he is the founder, composer, performer and graphic designer in the extreme metal band *"Stortregn"*, with whom he has already recorded four albums and played in three continents since 2005.

www.johansmith.net

www.facebook.com/johanguitare

Sables stellaires is recorded on the cd NAXOS:
Laureate Series - Winner, 2019 Guitar Foundation of America (GFA) Competition
Reference number :
8.574199

Other Mel Bay Classic Guitar Solo Books

24 Pieces for Guitar by Gilbert Isbin

25 Etudes Esquisses (Garcia)

A Tribute to Guitar Masters (Ramos)

Andrew York: 3 Dimensions for Solo Guitar

Anthology of Dimitri Fampas Music for Guitar (E. Fampas)

A Tribute to Guitar Masters (Ramos)

Classic Koshkin (Koshkin/Koonce)

Contemporary Anthology of Solo Guitar Music (Postlewate)

Contemporary Guitar Composers of the Americas (Multiple Authors)

Contemporary Pieces for Classical Guitar (Jakola)

Conversation Pieces (Long)

Diego Barber Compositions for Classical Guitar

Gordon Mizzi: Saints and Fireworks

Gordon Mizzi: Song of the Sea

Guitar Compositions by Carlos Dorado

Homage to Villa-Lobos and Other Compositions (Postlewate)

Introspect (Pellegrin)

Jazz Goes Classic (Multiple Arrangers)

Lyrical Solos (W. Bay)

Master Anthology of New Classical Guitar Solos (Multiple Composers)

Rock Goes Classic (Multiple Arrangers)

Solos for Guitar (F. Hand)

The Contemporary Guitar: An Anthology of New Music (S. Yates)

The Jovicic Collection (Dojcinovic)

Well Tempered Blues (Beauvais)